THOUGHTS
&
INSPIRATIONS

BITO DAVID

Thoughts and Inspirations

Poetry

THOUGHTS AND INSPIRATIONS

Bito David - bitodavid@gmail.com

ISBN-13: 978-0-9996530-0-5

Cover Design: Editions PerleDesAntilles
Layout: Editions PerleDesAntilles
Cover Picture: Izae

Editions PerleDesAntilles
7054 Chesapeake Circle
Boynton Beach, Florida 33436

Marin 12 # 7
Port-au-Prince, Haïti

perledesantilles1804@gmail.com
(561) 254-6043 / (509) 3116-8892

DEDICACE

To my circle of poets
Sharing with me this passion
To my circle of family members
And my circle of friends

To the circle of humanity

AUTHOR'S PREFACE

THOUGHTS! THOUGHTS! THOUGHTS! What good do they do to humanity? Ideas rule the world and dictate our way of life. On a daily basis the brain speculates and regurgitates a plethora of notions and theories.

Men are inspired by many visions that determine their philosophy. We think. We speculate. We define our realities based on conceptions imagined by a profusion of abstractions, hypotheses, and impulses.

Ideas rule the world and our life as well as our thoughts and inspirations.

555555555555

555555555555

THOUGHTS AND INSPIRATIONS

CONTENTS

8 AUTHOR'S PREFACE

12 A Man's Pride And Dignity
13 My Thoughts And My Lines
14 Naturally Sour Naturally Sweet
16 Dreamcatcher
17 Let It Be
18 You Want Love In Return
20 A Mother's Companionship
22 Bare Necessities
24 Believe In Your Dream
26 Bring It On Life
28 Butterfly In The Winds
29 Can You Fly My Life?
30 Dream (Don't Rely Always On Me)
32 Dependence And Freedom
33 Dressed Naked
34 Free The Birds Of Your Mind
35 Glory Of Life
36 I Am A Woman
37 I Can Fly Your Life

...9...

A MAN'S PRIDE AND DIGNITY

Don't compromise a man's sovereignty
And the foundations of his dignity
Don't erase the footprints of his glory
And the tenets of his history

A man's worth and pride
Is like the honor of a bride
The sanctity of her virginity
The virtue or her purity

Don't kill a man's dream
Of his train you'll curtail the steam
Don't beat his self-esteem
His river will lose its stream

A man's worth and pride
Is like the honor of a bride
It is his self-respect and his delight
The cause for which he should fight

MY THOUGHTS AND MY LINES

I am hiding behind the decor
On my bookshelf
But of these lines
I am the author

I am a free thinker
A liberate writer
I speculate my thoughts
With no goal to convert
The souls introverted

Those who wrote the gospels
And the ones repeating the messages
Have a stronger voice than mine
Echoing god's will and instructions
So they say so they wish

I propagate my speculations
For the sake of sharing with our creation
The elucubrations of a mind
Seeking a cosmic consciousness

NATURALLY SOUR NATURALLY SWEET

Naturally sour like a lime
Bitter like aloe all the time
Some souls while useful
Cannot be sweet and joyful

We must learn to love them
Treating their nature with kindness
We must learn to accept them
To fulfill our togetherness

Naturally sweet like honey
Simply kind like Barney
Other spirits remain cool
Even when facing the fool

Mother Nature created diversity
An amazing mosaic of plurality
Where the ultimate duality
Characterizes our humanity

Are you a lime
All the time
Are you sweet like honey
Bringing savor to the journey

Human nature is so divergent
One day cruel another clement
One day author of the worst crime
Another the jewel of the precious time

Naturally sour like lime
Bitter like aloe all the time
Naturally sweet like honey
Simply kind like Barney

DREAMCATCHER

I caught a dream
On the wings of time
Flying with a velocity
That transcends my reality

I caught a dream
That flourishes through time
A bouquet of happiness
With petals of togetherness

I caught a dream
While it was at its prime
Decorating the alleys of humanity
With the jewels of humility

I caught a dream
On the wings of time
With its pinions I fly
And of sadness I will never cry

LET IT BE

Let it be
Whether it's certain or maybe
Cut the lawn
Watch the dawn
Awaking a new day
And always find your way
Through the tragedy
Of life's mystery

Let it be
And your time will be
A source of energy
A breeze of symphony
That will soothe your melancholy
The pains of your disharmony
And the desert of your monotony
For eternity

YOU WANT LOVE IN RETURN

Can you feel the pain
And the harsh suffering
That my soul is bearing
When my flesh is hurting
And deep inside you wound me
You want love in return

Can you feel my sorrow
When my child is murdered
My brother is butchered
When my life is destroyed
And my hope is shattered
You want love in return

Your preachers continue
To teach me the virtue
Of pliant forbearance
Turning the other cheek
Every time you slap me
You want love in return

Can you feel the reality
Of my life in ignominy
My existence in poverty
All my days in anxiety
Enduring your tyranny
You want love in return

Your preachers instruct me
To abide with forbearance
To your evil and your wickedness
My misery one day will end
In the garden of paradise
With God's love in return

A MOTHER'S COMPANIONSHIP

I feel safety
In the comfort
Of your warm presence
That fills my essence

I feel peace
And my heart exults
When your tenderness
Softens its sadness

My world blossoms
And my home is a kingdom
Where your kindness reigns
Its power of grace

I feel loved
Every time your eyes
Connect with my sight
In a flash so bright
That rejoices my soul

Gone but not done
You still work your ways
To protect my days
Your spirit always
Watches over me

BARE NECESSITIES

Air and water
Food and shelter
Are in the decor of nature
But we look in our culture
For many artificial values
To spice up our menus

Human greed
Has an ego to feed
From the river of its many needs
Flow the torrents of its vile deeds
The wants it must justify
Are often not easy to qualify

It spurs ideologies
And a plethora of theories
To control the psychology
And establish hegemony
On a herd an oligarchy
Wishes to mystify the destiny

Air and water
Food and shelter
Are in the decor of nature
But we look in our culture
For many artificial values
To spice up our menus

BELIEVE IN YOUR DREAM

The dream in your mind
Is not impossible to achieve
You just need the ability to find
A very good reason to believe

Believe in your dream
And stay steadfast on the stream
That carries your boat to your success
Don't take no break no recess

The dream in your mind
Should be the goal of your life
Whether you face obstacles of any kind
Don't be afraid to confront the strife

Believe in your dream
Fly high and do not even scream
When you're about to reach the star
In your sky that seemed so afar

Believe in your dream
And keep heating up the steam
That fuels your determination
To accomplish your aspiration

The dream in your mind
Is not impossible to achieve
You just need the ability to find
A very good reason to believe

BRING IT ON LIFE

I never asked for storms
Acts of God
On a path of destruction
The weather's fantasies
Cripple us with cold
And sizzle us with heat

I never asked for the pains
And the hate blood in my veins
They say it's because of my sins
That my welfare is already ruined
But I did not create that conscience
Who fell into such bad negligence

Why are those viruses
Infecting my body
Killing me softly
Torturing my being
With their malignant presence
Compromising my existence

I was born with many passions
Sentiments and emotions
Boiling with exasperation
The calmness of my days
Did I invent them
To fulfill their mayhem

Why in a short life
I have to confront
The greatest challenges
Which ultimately
Leave me with dismay
Great pains and anguish

Bring it on life
What else do you have
To spoil my happiness
I know it is hell
The final torture
Bring it on if it is your pleasure

BUTTERFLY IN THE WINDS

It has wings
But likes the winds
And loves to fly free
Gliding with no fear
Through the air of liberty
And the space of humanity

It has wings
But it lets go
Whenever the breeze
Of life in its majesty
Carries its dreams
To the heights of infinity

Butterfly in the wind
Butterfly spreading its wings
Watch for the birds
Watch for your predators
While enjoying the breeze
While tasting your freedom

CAN YOU FLY MY LIFE

Can you fly my soul
Through the skies
Of an endless happiness
Like the clouds
Like the smoke
Shapeless vapors of time
Filling the widest gap

Can you fly my life
In a roller coaster ride
With the flow of your tenderness
Making my days everyday
A testimony of euphoria
A trip to the highest glory
On the road to eternity

Can you fly my life
While holding the string
Of my little kite
And not letting go

DREAM (Don't REly Always on Me)

Don't rely always on me
For your realities
Don't rely always on me
For one day I won't be here
Don't rely always on me
For my days are very short

To fully live your life
In harmony with its mysteries
Dream

Dream
Dream big
Dream loud
Dream white
Dream black
Dream brown
Dream in all colors

Life is worth a treasure
Dream to dig its value
Dream to create
The environment that will blossom
The garden of all your moments

Dream in your sleep
Dream with your eyes open
Dream while riding
The current of the river
That carries your hopes

Dream Dream Dream
And wake yourself up
With the realities of your desires

DEPENDENCE AND FREEDOM

Dependence is free
Cause it is easy
To make all types of
Allegiance to theories
Of alienation
Allegiance to gospel
For veneration
Allegiance to creed
And subornation

Dependence is free
A herd of brainless souls
With no transcendental knowledge
Follow the prescribed path
Designed by an oligarchy
To control their destiny

But freedom is costly

DRESSED NAKED

I am naked in my best costume
Wearing the skin of my reality
Dressed with the derma of my identity
With no feather no duvet no plume

I have no mask to cover my face
Easily one can find my trace
The great virtue of honesty
Is the tenet of my personality

I have no veil no box to hide
I always show my only pride
In the essence of my culture
And the substance of my nature

I am naked in my best costume
Only the smell of my perfume
Exudes from me an odd odor
I always wear my true colors

FREE THE BIRDS OF YOUR MIND

Free the birds of your mind
And destroy the railings of the cage
That prevent your spirit to rise

Open the wings of your brain
To the winds of a higher consciousness
That will drive you to the top altitude

If it's true that some birds walk
Many others proudly fly
And a few soar like eagles in the sky

If it's true that some souls crawl
Many others imperiously surge
May yours be among those that glide

Free the birds of your mind
And destroy the railings of the cage
That prevent your spirit to rise

GLORY OF LIFE

What is your philosophy
What guides the path of your destiny
Death with dignity
Is the pinnacle of humanity

Life in misery
Is an abject ignominy
Ignorance is an agony
That keeps the brain in poverty

Nobody will give you a trophy
If you don't overcome the adversity
Never beg for sympathy
Fight for your nobility

Life has no glory
When you relinquish your liberty
Your brain has validity
When you think for your autonomy

I AM A WOMAN

I am a woman
Of flesh and bones
Of heart and soul
Of a spirit of love
And a nature of goodness

I am a woman
And I carry on the stream
Of the flow of my dreams
The fleet of humanity
That I make float with dignity

I am a woman
With shoulders of iron
And feelings of fur
My tears and my blood
Fertilize the whole world

I am a woman
The complement of man
In the garden of the universe
I spread graciously the aroma
Of the charm of my beauty

I CAN FLY YOUR LIFE

I can fly your life
As high in the sky
Where the big rainbow
Shines its bright colors
On our lands of love

I can fly your life
Away from the strife
Of your emotions
And your commotions

I can fly your life
And not letting go
Till eternity
Fills your destiny

I can fly your life
In the deep heaven
With my strings of love
My winds of pleasure
Charming your fancies

I CAUGHT A RAINBOW

I caught a rainbow
In the sky of my happiness
Its colors reached so low
That I felt their tenderness

I felt the savor of its blue
Like the taste of the morning dew
Its red like the blood of my stream
Irrigated the lands of my dream

On my route its bright yellow
Seemed to be a happy path to follow
Orange green indigo and violet
Around my neck formed a nice chaplet

I caught a rainbow
Drinking in a fountain down below
It landed on earth to give me pleasure
And its treasures my heart nurture

I HAVE SEEN THOSE MASKS

I have seen those masks in my nightmares
Scary vampires bloodsuckers and criminals
Ugly men killers serving the dreadful agenda
Of an oligarchy that controls their empty brains

I have seen those masks in my nightmares
Below the curtain of their wickedness
Are the evil faces of the worst monsters
Trust me they are not human

I have seen those masks in my nightmares
And I always wake up in tears
Boogeymen marching in the streets
With uniforms and weapons of terror

I have seen those masks in my nightmares
Haunting my dreams of a better night
Destroying the beauty of a better tomorrow
Trust me they are not human

I MISS YOUR SOUL

It is dark in my heart
And my mind wanders in solitude
No bright stars in my sky
I miss your soul

Can you feel the cold
That freezes my blood
My senses become dumb
Cause I miss your soul

Can you hear me sob
The echo of my pains
Longing for your love
I do miss your soul

It is dark in my heart
And I feel loneliness
My eyes in tears cry
I miss your soul

INJUSTICE ANYWHERE

Injustice anywhere
Is injustice everywhere

The grief of a colony
Victim of a tyranny
Repression and cruelty
From an oligarchy
Is the grief of humanity

Injustice anywhere
Is injustice everywhere

The convergence of our actions
And our determination
Towards a pledge of emancipation
From subordination
And domination
Should be our motivation

Injustice anywhere
Is injustice everywhere

IT SHOULD NOT BE ALL ABOUT ME

It's all about me
Ego pride and narcissism
Selfishness and personal vanity
Sometimes my view of the world
Seems to be limited to my mirror

Should it be all about me
When there are all these identities
In the mosaic of humanity
Spreading their own personalities
In the universe of diversity

I often ignore their dignity
With the blinder of my presumptions
Measuring their realities
By my reduced personal dimensions
Self-centered around my definition

It should not be all about me
Life in its plurality
Shines with better clarity
The lights of the whole universe
Of which I am only a sparkle

LESSONS FROM FERGUSON

From the streets of Ferguson
I am hiding my son
Young black
From the wrong pack
Skin dark
Fresh meat for a shark

In the streets of our community
We must restore sanity
Dignity and respectability
Safety in our society
For the lives of humanity
By any means necessary

Young black
Skin dark
Meat for the shark
When driven off track
A young and respectful black
But his skin is dark

JUST BE STRONG

From the colonizers' speeches
To the preachers' sermons
The threat is death
If you don't accept

When towards the majesty
We don't show our loyalty
The menace is agony
In hell prison and captivity

When we don't pledge our allegiance
To the symbols of domesticity
The control mechanism
Is the propagation of fear
To terrorize our mind and body

The catalysts are ignorance
Low level of consciousness
And an abysmal mental deficiency

Just be strong
Just be brave

The remedies are our transcendence
Our excellence our self-emancipation
And our freedom of thought

Bravery is the quality
That will help us face the adversity
In the toughest realities

OUR STATE OF HUMANITY

In our state of humanity
The hardest language is veracity
The toughest challenge is honesty
The greatest difficulty is humility

Whether or not we affirm with certainty
To follow the path of magnanimity
We always fail in our tenacity
To overcome the adversity

Many lose their dignity
And allow an oligarchy
To control their destiny
Seemingly for eternity

Today our world society
Is led by a clan of greedy
The proudest lands are like Haiti
The others function in servility

A docile herd applauds this reality
For their benefits and with cruelty
Permitting the opulence of a minority
To cripple forever a vast majority

What an irony
The tenets of the universality
Of human's rights of equality
Is stepped over by a tyranny

NATURE OF ILLUSION

Catch your dream
While it is flying
Like a bird following your stream
If not your wonders will be dying

Catch your dream
When you are sleeping
Find the stream
When you are awaking

If life has a nature of illusion
It also can brighten your vision
And fulfill your aspirations
On the journey of your destination

Catch your dream
And follow the stream
That replenishes your essence
And nurtures your quintessence

OUR WORLD IS IN OUR MIND

Our world is in our mind
Creation of our imagination
Our perceptions and inhibitions
Our fears and apprehensions

Our world is in our mind
Shaped by our sagacity
And our sense of magnanimity
Towards the whole humanity

The world in our mind
Will be an inferno or a bad spell
When we deviously dwell
In our plans to make it a hell

The world in our mind
Will be a heaven or a shining light
When our thoughts are right
And our perceptions bright

PIECES OF DREAM

I cut life in many pieces
Half dreams half realities
But the pieces of dream
Follow the strongest streams

What carries our reveries
In this world of illusions
Our realities create confusion
Our dreams shape our vision

What makes our boat float
On this ocean of uncertainties
Our existence has mysteries
Plagued by many miseries

I cut life in many pieces
Half dreams half realities
But I rely on my fantasies
To fulfill my ecstasies

SIMPLE HUMAN COMPLEX REALITY

Simple human
Complex reality
Whether man or woman
The same humanity

Simple human
Subjugated by necessity
His weaknesses he can't ban
They come in a wide variety

Simple human
Whether man or woman
You and I we face the same fatality
Of existence in its complexity

Simple human
And none of us can
Change our humanity
Victim of our identity

SOCIAL HYPOCRISY

If you want to be popular
Just go with the flow
Of the crowds that follow
The path of the liar

If you dream to become famous
Just applaud the philosophy
That goes with the prescribed theology
And remain all the time credulous

Our world acknowledges
Those who live on the edges
Of humanism and common sense
And propagate its nonsense

Our society reserves a prime
To those who commit the vile crime
Of mystifying the intelligence
Of the masses with their science

If you wish to have followers
And on your grave so many flowers
Just repeat the grim litany
Of the world oligarchy

But if you choose to be honest
And with pride you do your best
Your reward will be modest
And glory never your guest

SPEAK OUT LOUD

Would you sign your name
Under a petition
For our martyrs' liberation

Would you sing the song
Of freedom and self-determination
For our race's emancipation

Would you speak out loud
Against exploitation
To stop our subordination

Would you join the rank
Of the crowd in protestation
Against discrimination

Or would you rather remain silent
Living your life in abjection
For fear of retribution

Always there to corroborate
The unjust system of our society
For the sake of your safety

But you would say the pledge
Of allegiance with no knowledge
It is not your plea not your anthem

In all situations
Silence in front of injustice
Is the strategy of an accomplice

A man with integrity
Will fight for human's dignity
By any means necessary

SOUL SEX

Soul sex is the connection
That unites two lovers in their passion
Where in a symbiosis of the emotions
Their minds and bodies merge their infatuation

Soul sex transcends the process
Of lovemaking in its recess
Where the spirits experience the endless caress
That provides the greatest intenseness

Love in its glorious dimension
Unites the psyches of human's sensations
In a profound and supreme satisfaction
Beyond the realm of their expectations

Soul sex is the union
Of the cosmos in communion
That reaches the sublime ecstasy
In a perfect state of harmony

TAKE AWAY MY FEARS

Take away my fears
Don't fill me with tears
I want my whole life
To be free of strife

But a flow of screams
Inundates my dreams
Life will never be
The milk of a bee

The gods you worship
Should be part of your mythology
Never embark on a ship
That does not carry your genealogy

The gods you worship
Must protect your ship
Take away your fears
And dry up your tears

THE PRICE OF FREEDOM
(A Tribute to Malcolm X)

The price of freedom
Is paid in a martyrdom

No screaming for mercy
No kneeling for amnesty
No begging for charity
No marching for clemency
No bowing for leniency
No asking for pity

To conquer his liberty
And preserve his dignity
To enjoy his nobility
Facing the tyranny
Of an oligarchy
Against humanity
A man needs bravery

The price of freedom is death
A fight until your last breath

THE WALL OF THE VILLAGE

I write on my wall
The lines of my life
No questions asked
No lessons taught
It is just a wall
For the graffiti
Of my creations
My imagination
My speculations

The wall of the village
Sees the venting spree
Of many emotions
Many pretentions
Many aspirations
Many illusions
Many inhibitions
That fed live
Our greed to humanity

THINK BRAIN THINK

Think brain think
Observe ponder and analyze
Don't swallow the prescribed theories
Established to control your psychology

Your value is in the originality
Of the thoughts that you can conceive
Without relying on others' suggestions
If not in a body you have no reason

Think brain think
Glorify the personality
Of the makeup where you reside
All the others have their own mind

Don't repeat the childish theories
Like Santa and all the flawed stories
You need to grow your perspective
Once gullible your reason needs to flourish

WEAPONS OF MASS DISTRACTION

Besides the weapons of mass destruction
There are the weapons of mass distraction
Entertainments and various comedies
Sitcoms that play so many weird parodies

The media broadcasts everyday
A plethora of propagandas that convey
The messages the rulers want to play
To softly divert their prey

They are the tools that the strong clan
Uses to implement his specific plan
Of alienation and mystification
In order to consolidate its domination

They are the weapons of mass distraction
More potent than those of destruction
They baffle subliminally our mind
Against them a recourse is hard to find

WHEN DEATH CALLS

When death calls
The coward hides
His predator
Fulfills his crime
With ease and pride

When death calls
The brave man fights
He stands and faces
His destiny
With dignity

When death calls
The weakling cries
Fearfully prays
Turning his face
Against his fate

When your death calls
Be strong and bold
Stand up and hold

Your pride as man
It's worth your balls

When my death calls
Remind me all
To stand my ground
Where once I preach
Not to breach

TO EVERY BIRD AND BEE

To every bird and bee
That flew in my garden
You brought a freshness
That revives my life

To every butterfly
That sucked my nectar
The sugar of my soul
You made my source flow

To those who sincerely
Share their warmth with me
I owe you my joy
And the depth of my happiness

To those who inspired
The muse of my dreams
My lines are for you
A tribute of love

I HAVE NEVER SEEN A BLACK ANGEL

My mind is puzzled with this marvel
Cause I have never seen a black angel
It seems that my sight is so pure
It transforms black into white for a cure

I have never seen a black angel
My color is on the face of the devil
My race is an abomination
Nowhere in the bible is its allusion

My delusional faith in a deity
Whose deputies are not of my identity
Seems to be a foolish abnormality
But my people believe this oddity

I have never seen a black angel
In my dreams dark visions are evil
My race is an abomination
But my brothers swallow this aberration

WHY SHOULD I FORGET

Why should I forget
The scars in my memory
That undignified my humanity

Why should I dismiss
The dark side of my history
That compromised my identity

I will never relinquish
My right to liberty
And my droit to dignity

I will never beg
For mercy and pity
When I face adversity

Why should I pardon
The villainies of a wicked faction
When God reserves evil a retribution

Why should I tolerate
The perpetuation of an ignominy
That disabled my community

Never will I forget
Never will I dismiss
My dream to live with integrity

THE CROWD THE HERD THE MASS

The crowd is the assembly
Sitting quietly at the temple
Obedient and full of faith
Never daring to question
The sermon that it is given

The herd is the multitude
Of the sheep under the control
Of a single running dog
Quietly it follows the path
Of this inciting leader

The mass is a populace
A mindless troupe of livings
A battalion that flocks like a swarm
An army of witless soldiers
A manipulable group of beings

Are you from the crowd
The herd or the populace
Are you part of the pack

Shadowing the track of a trendsetter
Are you from the mass
Under the power of the ruling class

A silent horde we always find
A set inert dumb and so blind
Their world is free from engagement
Whether it is or disappears
No difference in the world appears

Are you among the mute
The speechless souls facing the fools
Are you docile and compliant
Amenable and acquiescent
Always passive and submissive

So many want to teach you
So many want to lead you
So many want to control you
So many want to use you
So many want to abuse you

YOU ARE MY RAINBOW

You are my rainbow
The brilliant colors
That garnish my yard
And flourish my land
With petals of love

You are my rainbow
The songs of my blues
My wine pure and red
My greenest pasture
My mellow nature
Violet and yellow

You are my rainbow
To you my heart bows
My feelings explode
A blossom of joy
That fulfills my dreams

A GOOD FATHER'S LIFE

From an unconditional dedication
To mother children and wife
To a natural obligation
To vigorously suffer the daily strife
A good father's mission
Is always a heavy obligation

Even when misunderstood
For his family he always stood
Carrying the load of his responsibility
Performing to the best of his ability

A father's life is also a long fight
To earn respect for his dedicated plight
He must face the misdeeds of some compeers
Who abandon their mission for their beers
This for a reason or another
Affects the group altogether

Fathers of yesterday today and tomorrow
Your deeds are examples your sons will follow
Keep your leadership role intact
Be always the best leader of the pack

BE ME BE YOU

Be me like I am you
In a symbiosis of passion
Where our egos resemble
The marriage of night and day

Be in me like I am in you
Melting our whole existence
In a pot of love connection
From a higher dimension

Be you and let me be me
In our particular originality
So we have to each other
Something original to offer

Be you and I will be me
With the pride of an identity
That makes our humanity
The jewel of plurality

BE THE POEM

No more words of dreams
On my virtual page
No more fantasies
In my world of desire

Be the poem
And pour your ink
On the fibers of my skin
Inundating my flesh
With the sweet stream
Of your savory sap
Let your inspiration
Please my sensations
And my deep emotions

Be the poem
That fills my phantasms
Be the melody
That rocks my whole body

CONTEMPLATION

I have a connection with life
And the marvels of its creations
I have an intimacy with the cosmos
And the mystery of its existence
What do I know
I just feel
And just kneel
But not in adoration
But rather in contemplation
Of the plethora of the enigmas
That blow my mind
And my intelligence
In consternation

I want to live the symbiosis
That would let me fuse
My reality and my conscience
With the essence
Of this majestic universe
With no ego
With no self

No I
Just kneeling
In contemplation
Mesmerized and puzzled
In front of this big secret
Unknown by man

I have a connection with life
And the marvels of its creations
I have an intimacy with the cosmos
And the mystery of its existence

DAILY WRITER

Like the common preacher
I am a daily writer
But my stances are not an ideology
Prescribed by a holy clergy
Controlling a theocracy
For the hegemony
Of an aristocracy

I am a daily writer
But far from a recruiter
Of adepts and followers
My garden grows other flowers
My speeches are philosophies
Emanating from the theories
Of a free thinker

I am a daily writer
Pouring the flow of my water
With no egocentric intentions
Sharing just my speculations

WHAT ARE YOU BUILDING

We want to build the premises of unity
Mutual agreement for solidarity
For the orientation of our humanity
Toward a sublime goal of fraternity

We want to build a bridge of humanism
To connect the islands of our egoism
A path along which the world community
Will be able to walk in harmony

We want to build the foundations
On which to erect a construction
That will accommodate our differences
On a large land without fences

What are you building with your vision
Are they walls or fences of division
If you are willing to share our resources
There will be no need for these discourses

EITHER DJANGO OR UNCLE TOM

Your speech defines you
Your thoughts identify you
One understands by your ideology
The background of your philosophy,

Your actions typify you
Your reactions characterize you
You are either Django proud fighter
Or Uncle Tom ignoble flatterer
Unchained or brainwashed
A free mind or a spirit enslaved

When you negotiate your dignity
And applaud cowardly the ignominy
You are Uncle Tom
When you can't stand with courage
Against the vile acts of outrage
But rather try to justify
The atrocities of the oligarchy
You are Uncle Tom

When you preach the gospel
That put a nasty spell
Over your people and nation
To keep them in abomination
You are Uncle Tom

When you believe in the theories
That destroy your communities
And criticize the champions
Who fought for your emancipation
You are Uncle Tom

You should be a proud Django
Like our heroes a long time ago
Who accepted the price to pay
To bring freedom our way

You should be a proud Django
Like our martyrs a long time ago
Who died for our liberation
And the independence of our nation

I WANT TO DROWN MY SOUL

I want to drown my soul
In the waters of your dreams
I want to draw my soul
In the chaos of your screams

I will navigate my boat
On the lake of your tears
You will be the precious coat
To warm up my fears

I will not shiver
As long as you and I can see
Like a wet beaver
I will swim in your sea

I want you queen of heart
To cure the illness of my passion
You're my darling sweetheart
Of my life an infatuation

I want to reach your horizon
To find the healing of my pain
Giving my life a reason
To believe it is not in vain

I want to drown my soul
In the waters of your dreams
To find a wave really cool
To quench my hottest steams

SHAME TO HUMANITY

When you lie to humanity
In support of the atrocity
Of a vile oligarchy
You are an ignominy

When you side with the anarchy
Of a small minority
That subdues a majority
Your action is a cruelty

When you have the capacity
To champion veracity
But echo only falsity
Your standard is audacity

When you use your authority
To commit barbarity
With no heart but just bigotry
You are a shame to humanity

You should use your hegemony
The leadership of your supremacy
To instill in our society
A world order of magnanimity

When you use your psychology
To alienate a group without mercy
For the sake of an autocracy
You are a shame to humanity

You should know your identity
You came up with the philosophy
Of control and ascendancy
Over my community

You should use your authority
The power of your hegemony
The tenets of your philosophy
To enhance our reality

SO MANY OF OUR MEN AND WOMEN

So many of our men
Unfortunately have lost their brain
They still cannot unchain
The strings of their intellectual pain

So many of our men
Cannot use their own pen
To write the pages of their history
They rely on the oligarchy

There are men and women
Who over the years hardly can
Ascertain the roots of their identity
They accept the lies of others' history

So many of our men
So many of our women
Sell their soul and their dignity
To a vile sovereignty

WHILE I FEAST ON THANKSGIVING

While I feast today
And give thanks to God
Is he sharing the wealth
Of our humanity
With the starving souls
Is it their own choice
Does he seem to care
Can he see their plea
The faithful can explain
That his plan is perfect

While I feast today
And in my faith I pray
Millions are starving
A world is dying
But my gospel teaches
They will go to hell
They don't have the grace
Of the supreme king

LINEAR CYCLICITY

The evidence shows that infinity
Functions in a linear cyclicity
The sun rises and sets daily
The moon follows it regularly
The tides of the sea simply
Continue the moves of its destiny
On the beach they irrigate constantly
And the boats of our life float quietly

Life goes around and around
In a mystery so profound
That puzzles our intelligence
And confounds our deep science

The concept of simple linearity
Seems congruent with monotony
It takes the variable of rotation
To make sense of the universe's equation

SHATTERED DREAMS

When a bird loses his wings
Suddenly vanish
His joy of flying
And his pride to be free

When a boy loses his legs
With them goes his freedom
The tools of his mobility
The dream of his humanity

It is sad in our world
That many limbs are gone
With them joy and freedom
Become only wishful dreams

When a bird loses his wings
When a boy loses his legs
What a sadness for humanity
To see their world in such agony

KNOWLEDGE IS POWER

Like a beautiful flower
Blooming on the field
Of a fertile garden
Watered by the sky
Lightened by the sun
Nourish your brain
With the best nutrients
Of a good education

Knowledge is power
Education is the key
It gives the upper hand
In the battle of big ideas
For greater accomplishments

Knowledge is power
Education is the key
It is obtained by the training
Of the mind to excellence
Learning life's art and science

Like a beautiful flower
Blooming on the field
Of a fertile garden
Watered by the sky
Lightened by the sun
May your brain cells prosper
May your intellect conquer
The frontier of all cognition

THE TENTACLES OF ALIENATION

The tentacles of alienation
Are numerous in their action
In our brain and in our mind
They will intelligently find
A failure a weakness
In our thoughts they bring distress
Around our ankles and our wrists
If we don't have two strong fists
The will impose their ugly chains
That will cause us so many pains

The tentacles of alienation
Expand widely their domination
They are economic policies
They are political strategies
They are subliminal
They are psychological
They are mental
They are spiritual

They are cultural
They are intellectual

The tentacles of alienation
Are numerous in their action
The tentacles of alienation
Expand widely their domination

AUTHOR'S POSTFACE

Poetry is the expression
Of the soul in its vibrations
It is a flow of thoughts
A shower of words
A passionate current
Of the eruption of ideas
One day by a conventional verb
With its artistic expression
And the other by a simple slang
With its aesthetic nature

Like the effusion channel
Of deep and sound feelings
It conveys at the same time
A sublime and exalted flood
Of love and humanism
Affection and altruism

Commitment and activism
Exciting positivism
In the visionary phrases
Of an artist's verbose lines

Poetry is a clear stream
That fills the hungry crucibles
With elevated emotions
Intimate confidences
Exciting exchanges
And intense speculations
Poetry is in the identity
Of the essence of humanity
In its garden of imagery
The dreams all the time wander
In words and lines and sounds
That frame the perceptions of the world

ABOUT THE AUTHOR

Bito David is an intellectual activist who uses his writing to convey a social message of humanism, patriotism, philosophy, realism and love. His words and his lines follow the inspiration of a total free thinker. His ideas are the deep and open speculations of the human brain trying to connect with the larger humanity for a deeper sense of existence and the fantasies of time and space along with the circumstances in life.

.